If You Only Knew

Revealing the Humanity of Mental Illness

Interviews and Photographs

by Barb Kellogg

Nothing in this book should be considered medical advice or guidance. A list of resources is located at the end of this book. All participants interviewed agreed to appear in this book. Some names were changed at the participant's request.

First Printing 2019

23 22 21 20 19   5   4   3   2   1

ISBN: 978-1-946195-50-0
Library of Congress Number: 2019917622

Photography and Interviews by Barb Kellogg

Printed in the United States
Published by FuzionPress
1250 E 115th Street, Burnsville, MN 55337

Interior formatting by Ann Aubitz FuzionPress.com
Cover design by Barb Kellogg

Contents

Preface: How It All Began

I created *If You Only Knew* from a place of kind curiosity and openness to understanding.

The idea for the photo essay was inspired by conversations with a friend who battled depression. Those conversations helped me understand the illness. Not the textbook definition of it. But how it actually *felt* in terms I could relate to.

After that experience, I wondered how I could use my talent and insight as a photographer to visually translate personal descriptions of mental illness. Perhaps helping others better understand mental illness as well.

In the beginning, I envisioned this project as an art exhibit, hoping to share interviews, portraits, and visual analogy photographs featuring about ten people. To my surprise, ten people quickly agreed to be interviewed. And then that number easily grew to fifteen, the maximum I felt the exhibit space could accommodate.

I was astonished. Not only were people sharing pieces of their personal—and sometimes challenging—experiences with mental illness, but most were willing to have their portrait taken as part of the photo essay.

You might wonder, as I did, why anyone would share their personal story so publicly. When I asked participants this question, some common themes shaped their responses. Jenna's and Chelsea's interviews reflect these themes. Jenna hoped to break down the stigma of mental illness—"To do that, you have to talk about it," she said. Chelsea shared her story in "hopes that it will help just one person."

At some point, I made the decision to continue conducting interviews and creating portraits despite not needing more for the exhibit. I explained to these extra participants that I *might* do a book in the future.

The photo essay received a wonderful response at the art exhibit, so my decision to move forward with this book was relatively easy.

A total of thirty-two people agreed to be interviewed, including those already a part of the exhibit. People found out about the project in several ways: from my initial request for interviews, from friends of people I'd interviewed, and from me talking about the project at art events.

I've created a vignette for each participant, combining each interview with either a portrait or a visual analogy photograph, or both. The text and photographs are meant to complement one another, telling a richer story than one element could tell alone.

During interviews, I asked a series of questions to learn about each person's journey. The central question was, "What does your mental illness feel like?" The participants' responses were the creative impetus for the visual analogy photographs.

I created most of the visual analogies specifically for their respective interviews, and I selected a few from my photo archives when I had an image that I felt perfectly interpreted someone's feelings. Nature plays a featured role, as I believe it makes the topic of mental illness more relatable and approachable.

In addition to visual analogies, there are portraits in the book. It was important for me to include them in order to further humanize *If You Only Knew* and let the readers see that mental illness can happen to anyone. The creation of each portrait was a collaboration between the participant and me, with the goal being authenticity. No one was directly asked to smile, so the range of captured expressions reflect the many faces we all present to the rest of the world.

In book form, *If You Only Knew* can be experienced by more people than those visiting the art exhibit. And by reaching more people, it can further realize my original goals: to create a bridge of understanding between those with and without mental illness, to decrease stigma and discrimination, to increase awareness about the experience of mental illness, and ultimately to humanize it.

Acknowledgments

It took a village to make this book a reality. I wish I could list everyone. The words *gratitude* and *thank you* seem insufficient, but know I mean them sincerely.

To everyone I interviewed: This book is dedicated to all of you. I am grateful beyond words that you trusted me to share your stories.

Kyle: For believing in me and always standing by me—I love you.

Mom and Dad: I love you for the lifetime of encouragement you've given me.

Leah: WAALFU ;) (She knows what it means.)

Linda: Thank you for *all* your help and for being a great sounding board.

Sue, my second-grade teacher: Thank you for your belief in me all these decades later.

Clients and staff of Hope Community Support Program (Catholic Charities, Saint Cloud, Minnesota): You were the first to join me on this project. Your support, encouragement, and trust mean the world to me. Together, we *can* make a difference.

North Hennepin Community College (Brooklyn Park, Minnesota): Tom, thank you for believing in this project and helping me reach a broader audience.

Thank you to all the friends—and even strangers—who offered words of encouragement over the course of this project. You'll never know how much I needed to hear them. And thank you to all who have supported me by attending my art events and sharing my work with other people.

Prior to writing this book, which is my first, I never understood why authors effusively thank their editor and publisher. But I get it now. Angie and Ann, *thank you* for your patience and guidance and for being part of this adventure.

Partial funding for both the art exhibit and book were made possible through grants from Central Minnesota Arts Board (Foley, Minnesota), thanks to funds provided by the McKnight Foundation.

Floral Arts (Saint Joseph, Minnesota): Elaine, your encouragement and collaboration was wonderful.

Paint Addict Studios (Minneapolis, Minnesota): Justin, thank you for printing the canvases for the exhibit. They were beautiful, as always.

Paramount Center for the Arts (Saint Cloud, Minnesota): Thank you for selecting the exhibit and providing the opportunity to debut it at Gallery St. Germain.

Introduction

Who Should Read This Book

If you're curious, it's OK—this book is for anyone who wants a sense of what it's like to walk in someone else's shoes. You can begin to discover what depression, schizophrenia, and other illnesses feel like through these authentic and powerful interviews and photographs.

If you've ever felt misunderstood or invisible, this book offers validation and encouragement.

If you're ready to help open the conversation around mental illness and fight the discrimination associated with it, this book will fuel your desire for change.

How to Read This Book

The interviews can be read in any order.

Please note that some of the content in this book may be emotionally difficult for sensitive readers.

What This Book Is Not

This is not a self-help book. Nor is it a book of medical advice or guidance, even though some participants share details and opinions about their treatment experiences. Please remember each person is unique. There is no one-size-fits-all approach to living with or experiencing mental illness.

This book does not represent *all* individuals living with mental illness. While I made efforts to interview people with varied backgrounds, it was never my intention to explore every mental illness and socioeconomic, racial, and ethnic circumstance.

This book is not a series of complete biographies. Each interview contains only a slice of each person's much-fuller life story. Limiting the scope of each interview to the central theme was one of the more difficult aspects of the process, yet it was necessary to keep the focus on what mental illness feels like.

What This Book Is

If You Only Knew is a photo essay depicting what mental illness feels like. It's an authentic and powerful collection of interviews and photographs that portray the humanity of mental illness.

If You Only Knew is about strength, humor, perseverance, vulnerability, heartbreak, and optimism.

If You Only Knew is ultimately about connection. About being seen. Being heard. Being understood. Everyone in this book was excited to share their story. Many shared with the hope of making the path easier for someone else. To anyone who has experienced mental illness—whether it be briefly or over a lifetime—they offer encouragement and validation.

The Vignettes

Bella, age 12
"Fuzzy and confusing . . ."

Bella is an articulate, deep-thinking, and mesmerizing teenager who **"wanted to be part of this photo essay so that others could better understand mental illness. . . . We are all different. Different maladies. Different things that go right and wrong. But you always have to try to understand others, because maybe one day it might happen to you."**

Bella remembers feeling anxious in response to her kindergarten teacher overreacting whenever Bella would answer a question incorrectly. A few years later, she experienced a lot of stomachaches. By fourth grade, her symptoms had escalated. She had visions of cutting herself, she would actually cut and bite herself, and she would rub an eraser on her skin to the point of pain—all to temporarily feel more whole and help the feelings of emptiness go away. She even thought about hurting other people, particularly her brother. It was at this point that Bella told her parents, because she **"knew things weren't right or healthy."**

Bella's parents have always been very supportive. Her mom's advice to other parents is to **"stay calm, keep your cool. 'Cause you won't help your kids if you overreact. Be their biggest advocate."** Early in the process, Bella received a misdiagnosis of schizoaffective disorder, depressive type. She was eventually diagnosed with and is receiving treatment for severe depression and generalized anxiety disorder. **"If it doesn't feel right,"** Bella's mom says, referring to diagnoses, **"keep searching for the answers."**

How does Bella's mental illness feel? **"Kind of like static or moving pixels. A sense of strangeness or something wrong. Like fuzzy and confusing. Nothing seems real. I go to my own mind and sometimes get trapped there."** She says one of the hardest things »

"Fuzzy and confusing . . ."

to explain is when it feels like something or someone is out to get her, even though no one is.

For Bella, the worst point came a few years ago, when she had extreme thoughts of hurting and killing herself. She sent a message to a friend's mom, saying goodbye. That parent called Bella's parents. It was a heart-wrenching experience for Bella's parents to see her admitted to the hospital. Bella says, **"I was nervous about it, partly caring, partly freaking out, part not caring."**

Life is easier now, but Bella didn't think she'd be in a good place this young. She's on medication that helps, and she sees a therapist and psychiatrist. **"I'm a lot better at dealing with emotions."** Drawing to express her feelings also helps her, as does listening to music and talking to her mom.

To other kids and adults, Bella says, **"Mental illness can happen at any age. No matter your experiences. No matter what you look like. You're still human. And brains are complex, with plenty of room for things to go wrong—where mental illness steps in. But just like a machine might not be completely fixed, you can still work on it. Your mental illness is like that."**

Betty, age 62
"Lost."

Betty has such kind eyes, is introspective, and speaks with a gentle, soft voice. **"There's hope,"** she says to people struggling with their mental illness. **"Talk to someone—keep talking until you find the hope. Be OK with just** *being* **for a while. Know that there are people who care and understand. Find those support groups—you'll find friendship and loyalty in them."** She also says to **"treat yourself like your best friend."**

Betty was diagnosed with depression and anxiety when she was fifty years old. She doesn't know why it started, as nothing specific happened in her life to trigger it. However, Betty can look back now and recognize the beginnings of milder symptoms decades earlier.

At its worst, she recalls feeling really tired, with fatigue so extreme she couldn't do anything. **"I'd sit in the recliner and look at the floor all day long."** Thoughts of suicide were a reality for her. Recollecting the experience, she says, **"It's difficult to describe how horrible it really was. And it was nobody's fault. It just happened out of the blue. It was great having people not give up on me."**

Betty's major turning point came as she was preparing to act on her suicide plan. She had the pills for an overdose, she had chosen the clothes to wear, and she had said her goodbyes to people. Before she was about to execute her plan, she called her husband, telling him goodbye. **"I can't do it anymore,"** she told him. Asking her to wait, he rushed home and took her to the emergency room.

Betty was hospitalized for two weeks. She then received partial treatment for another month. Her son got married during this time; Betty's memory of the wedding is a blur. She explains that she **"faked it so others would think I was OK."** »

"I felt so alone. Worthless," she says. This was why her husband's support **"meant everything"** to her. **"We'll fight this together,"** he told her. He started doing everything, including household chores. **"He was the greatest support. I couldn't have done all this. He just let me be. Which was what I needed."**

Betty describes her depression as feeling **"empty. Want to hide. Dark. Hopeless. Never ending."** She expands these ideas further, saying, **"It feels like I'm an ant on a white peony. I'm not worthy of color. In acres of peonies that no one can find. I'm lost in that. No one can find me . . . but I want to be found."**

To give you an idea of the depths her depression reached, Betty shares an emotional, raw excerpt from her journal:

> *I don't know how I got here. I'm out at sea, anchored to a buoy. . . . There is nothing to do. Hope? For what? The days pass. I feel no cold of night nor heat of day. . . . I may be thirsty. I'm not sure. Even if I am, I don't care. I am alone. . . . Sometimes, I wonder how long I must exist like this. How long can I? . . .*
>
> *Will I ever laugh? I won't cry anymore. I've cried for weeks and I've run out of sadness. Now I am just empty. Existing. Why? Why do I not die? . . . God has left me, but not left me. I know He is there but I no longer feel Him. Again . . . empty. Worthless. Hopeless. I have no energy to do anything. Just be. It hurts.*

Betty's depression and anxiety are better managed today and are generally easier to live with, but they can still be a struggle to overcome. For instance, sometimes making a decision about what to have for supper and then finding the energy to prepare it is a real hurdle. One of the things she does to cope is to reach out to one person every day. Betty's family was and continues to be supportive. It also meant a lot when coworkers warmly embraced her after she told them what was happening.

Working full-time isn't possible right now, but two days a week strikes the right balance. It gives her some motivation to get out of the house, yet it doesn't drain her energy level beyond what she can emotionally manage.

In particular, social situations are difficult. **"Interacting with people is a struggle. I used to draw energy from people before. But to fight for every smile is so hard. Tiring. You're acting. It draws your energy down."** As a young woman, Betty never thought she'd ever deal with these kinds of feelings. **"I'm not gregarious Betty anymore. Never thought I'd be an introvert."**

She describes how she was sitting at her kitchen table one day, thinking, ***"Will I ever get better?*** I knew there was hope. *God's time, not man's time. Will I live to see that, God?* Just silence. *How do I go from nobody to somebody again?* I still struggle with that."** This is why she asked that her portrait be out of focus. To her, it represents that **"I'm just a dim person of what I could be."** But at the same time, she wants her portrait to reflect **"that it could be anybody."** ✠

Brad, age 58
"A dark tunnel with light at the end."

For Brad, the hardest part of his schizophrenia is helping people understand it's an illness. **"I'm not strange. I'm just like you,"** he says. **"It's not curable, but like any other illness, it's manageable, with medication and support. The schizophrenia doesn't define me."**

Brad's schizophrenia and dissociative disorder were triggered by a traumatic brain injury due to an accident. For this reason, he doesn't feel he's experienced the same stigma associated with mental illness that others have. His diagnosis seems more acceptable to people because it was the result of the accident.

Stigma or no stigma, however, life for Brad used to be a big struggle. On bad days, the voices said awful things: they urged him to cut himself, they expressed hatred, and they told him to die. To Brad, it sounded as if the voices were outside his head, audible to everyone. Sometimes Brad couldn't get his own words out. Every thought was overwhelmingly bad, as if his brain were a clogged drain. In response to the voices, he would sometimes cut himself. **"When I cut, it shut up the negative voices. They wanted me to hurt myself, hate myself, cut myself. 'Shame! Die! Fear!' I didn't feel the emotional pain when I cut."** The act of cutting was the only control he had when everything else felt so out of control.

Brad relays how his mental illness has felt: **"A dark tunnel with light at the end. My life might have dark moments, but there were and are always bright moments."** Life is a lot better now for Brad. **"I got my cognitive [functioning] back—can think because of the right combination of meds and support."** On his good days, he loves to write music, play guitar, and just enjoy life. To keep himself at his best, Brad takes his medication and sticks with new ones long enough to give them a chance to work. He also has the love of his »

"A dark tunnel with light at the end."

sweetheart of over ten years, plus support from his kids, other family members, and his social worker.

To others living with mental illness, Brad encourages you to **"find something you're passionate about. To get involved with life again. If you can handle it, do something fun that excites you."** To friends and family of people living with mental illness, he says, **"It's OK to just sit with them, hug, or cry. Be understanding, loving, and patient."** ✠

Candace, age 42
"Hurt. Abandoned. Loneliness and uncertainty."

"My life has been hard due to personal choices," Candace says, **"but I've learned to reach out more. I don't let my mental illness define me. I choose to accept it. It has made me stronger. The biggest key has been getting help and taking care of myself."**

Candace lives with bipolar depression and is also a recovering alcoholic. Outside of her family, most people don't know about her mental illness. Despite being very private, however, she wants to share her story to lend her voice and quiet determination to this project. **"I want others to understand that people with mental illness are normal. We can survive. Don't judge us."**

Her symptoms began around age ten or eleven, but it took ten frustratingly long years before Candace received the formal diagnosis of bipolar depression when she was admitted to the state hospital. Prior to that, she had attempted suicide and been admitted to an inpatient mental health facility. This was also the time frame in which her alcoholism began, as drinking helped bury her emotional pain. After being in the state hospital, she received a court order to live in a group home. She embraced the opportunity, as it helped her learn how to cope and focus on herself.

Candace admits that life can still be difficult today because she's dealing with a lot of issues. When her husband died a couple of years ago, she sought help, even though she hadn't been to counseling for years. She also attends Alcoholics Anonymous more often.

Candace feels she has limits. Her mental illness has changed who she is. **"I feel like I have a lost soul. Hurt. Abandoned. It robbed me of my life. It's scary because I don't know when my life is going to be manic or depressed. I have feelings of loneliness and uncertainty, but it is slowly getting better." »**

"Hurt. Abandoned. Loneliness and uncertainty."

In particular, she feels her bipolar depression has its challenges. **"When in a manic state, people love the rush and throw their pills away. But that isn't the right thing to do, because the worst thing about being manic is the crash afterwards. You just lay in bed. Dishes on the floor."**

One of her low points in life was when she started a house on fire and went to jail. **"I didn't know what I was thinking."** Afterwards, Candace committed herself into a state hospital. To others dealing with a mental illness she says, **"It's OK to get help and reach out. Gotta take care of yourself to enjoy the life you were given to the best of your ability."**

Chelsea, age 30
"A thousand different pieces."

"We bleed just the same."

That's what Chelsea wants you to know about a person with a mental illness. She's sharing part of her story **"in hopes that it will help just one person."**

Chelsea has struggled with attentiveness throughout her life because she has attention-deficit/hyperactivity disorder (ADHD). As a mother, she catches herself not being mentally present with her daughter. ADHD makes Chelsea get **"hyperfocused on one thing, and if someone tries to distract me from that, I get so ticked."** Chelsea struggles more when she finds herself with competing tasks, as it's difficult to prioritize. For her, ADHD can create a sense that everything must be done immediately. That leads to feeling overwhelmed, and sometimes nothing gets done. Chelsea visualizes her ADHD as feeling like **"glass that has broken into a thousand different pieces."**

Chelsea's experience has fueled her to talk more about ADHD and the misperceptions about it. Uninformed people called her **"dumb, scatterbrained, or unorganized,"** which only drove her to graduate college with honors. Her perseverance to succeed with her coursework was reflected in her statement, **"I'm not going to give up until I do understand!"** Her time in college **"totally empowered"** her.

She utilized Access Services, where staff worked with her to design the special accommodations she needed to ensure equal access, such as a quiet testing area and extended test-taking time. To those who criticize her for having received what they consider special treatment, Chelsea quickly says, **"Oh no, you don't!"**

Chelsea's struggle to maintain focus is real. It's something she deals with daily, and she manages her ADHD in varied ways. She exercises daily, practices mindful alone time through prayer, and eats healthy. She discovered »

"A thousand different pieces."

that her **"emotions are a roller coaster if I eat junk food!"** Chelsea also sets up her environment for success, adopting a minimalist mindset and avoiding clutter.

Through it all, she has turned her struggle with ADHD into a positive, knowing that **"our processing to get to a solution is different than others', but we usually find an answer that exceeds expectations."** Even Chelsea didn't expect to be as successful as she is today. **"I'm in such a good place right now! I'm very blessed."**

And if you're reading this and struggling with your mental health, Chelsea offers encouragement: **"Don't give up on yourself. Dreams can become reality."** ✠

David, age 54

"You're no good."

David lives with bipolar depression and schizophrenia. Because of time and/or medication, the negative voices telling him **"you're no good"** aren't as prevalent as they used to be. David's advice to others in this situation: **"Don't listen to the voices if they're bad."** He sometimes goes to both individual and group therapy. David's mental illness prevents him from driving or working. He was homeless for a time, but he says his life is a bit better now, as he has a place to stay. ✻

DJ, age 45
"A roller coaster."

"It can feel like a roller coaster," DJ says of her mental illness. "I can go from ecstatically happy to wanting to be dead in a split second. And I don't see the mood changes coming."

Upon meeting DJ, you know you're talking with someone who is smart, has a biting wit, and cares about others. She has a complex list of diagnoses: bipolar depression, borderline personality disorder, severe anxiety, posttraumatic stress disorder, plus several more.

DJ attributes part of her mental illness to being molested as a child plus being a victim of severe physical abuse within her own family throughout childhood. "I've been in a lot of shitty relationships from childhood into adulthood," she says. As an adult, it's been difficult for her to recognize when she's making a bad decision.

She admits to being a self-medicator and often doesn't take her prescribed medication. "I get in trouble. That's how far life goes down the rabbit hole. It forces me to seek treatment, get back on meds and therapy." As for why she frequently gets off track and stops her meds, she says, "I get scared if things are getting too good. In the past, when great things happened, I got treated like shit. It becomes a self-fulfilling prophecy."

At first, DJ says life isn't easier today than when she was younger; rather, it's "just different." She explains, "I'm more informed now, but I feel more helpless." Later during the interview, she says her life overall is "shittier than what I had before. I don't want to be here, but I won't do that to my kids."

At the end of the interview, though, DJ's signature humor appears. "I get a new owner's manual with every annual psych evaluation. How many people come with an owner's manual?"

Eric, age 51

*"Sometimes overwhelming and lonely,
but sunshine makes everything better."*

"Some people don't think it's a disease. They say, 'You'll get over it.'" This is the hardest thing for Eric to communicate about his mental illness. **"It's hard to explain to different people what we go through. Some don't listen."**

Eric is a kind-hearted, gentle person who lives with major depression and chronic anxiety, in addition to long- and short-term memory problems due to a traumatic brain injury. His parents verbally abused him as a child, and his twin brother didn't want him around. Memories as well as present-day situations trigger his posttraumatic stress disorder.

In high school, Eric turned to drugs, then escalated to heavy drug use in his twenties. This put him in situations where he was sexually abused by other men.

Through it all, he always worked—he was a functional drug addict.

Eric has found some relationships difficult as an adult. A marriage ended in divorce. And even though he hasn't used illegal drugs for the past five years, some of his family still see him as the addict he was twenty years ago.

Like everyone, Eric has bad days and good—**"sometimes overwhelming and lonely, but sunshine makes everything better."** He admits that life is still a struggle, but he has a better way of handling the stress than in the past. Listening to gospel music and going to church are why he's sober today. **"God keeps blessing me despite my faults."**

"Sometimes overwhelming and lonely,
but sunshine makes everything better."

Gary, age 66
"A constant storm . . ."

On a bad day, especially in the past, Gary would describe his mental illness as **"feeling like a constant storm over me, with impending death and disaster, always looking for the worst."**

Gary is a well-dressed and well-spoken gentleman—smart, full of charm, and quick to smile. He lives with severe depression and borderline personality disorder. His life today is a testament to his strength and courage, as his past was full of violence in and outside of gangs. That lifestyle was all Gary knew growing up. Looking back, he figures his mental illness began when he was a kid. He believes he turned his depression into aggression because he didn't know what to do with his feelings.

These feelings didn't strike him as different until his wife died in 1986, when he couldn't come out of **"that funk."** He beat himself up emotionally and had suicidal thoughts. This led to him being in and out of mental health wards, and he drank excessively while on heavy antidepressants. Eventually admitted to a state hospital, Gary was able to drop his prescription drug use to lower levels. This helped him lead a better life.

His advice to others living with mental illness is to **"look ahead, go forward not backwards. There is life ahead. Do your medication. Don't stop because you think you're cured. Find someone to talk to so you can get your ya-yas out."**

To those unfamiliar with mental illness, Gary says, **"There's a difference between mental illness and retardation. There's a *difference*. The more you pick on a person with a mental illness, the more they put themselves down. We're human too."**

"A constant storm . . ."

James, age 72
"Haunting bad memories."

What has posttraumatic stress disorder (PTSD) felt like at times to James? **"A combination of haunting bad memories. They cause torment, and until you can get over that torment, the bad memories are there."** He had to learn to forgive others before he could begin to heal.

James is an army veteran who served in Vietnam and Cambodia from 1966 to 1967. However, he believes the biggest misconception about PTSD is that it affects *only* veterans. **"It can happen to anyone—a pastor, a therapist, a friend. Any trauma. Not just a soldier. It can be a combination of traumas on top of each other, seemingly innocent alone, but can add up to trouble."** He added, **"If you don't ask for help, you'll put yourself in a hole, and depend on [illicit] drugs or commit suicide to cope."**

He can trace the origin of his PTSD to two particular enemy attacks that occurred on the same day. This event didn't seem significant to him for a few years, though—he didn't immediately experience PTSD symptoms upon returning home.

After leaving active service, James started experiencing mild symptoms, but he felt they were manageable. Sometimes he'd get angry. Loud noises—such as fireworks and heavy rain—could trigger flashbacks to his war experiences. Other times, he thought he could hear running footsteps at night. **"Your first reaction is to freeze, until you recognize what's really happening,"** he explains. In his sleep, his arms would flail.

For thirty-six years, James did fairly well coping with his PTSD without professional help. He primarily attributes this to the fact that he had two special support people in his life. He would openly share his most private emotions with them, often for hours at a time. »

"Haunting bad memories."

Other times, solitude helped him manage stress. **"I enjoyed being by myself and would often take my boat out and be gone for the day."** He also chose jobs where he could be alone on the road driving.

But within seconds, James's life changed dramatically in 2005. At age fifty-nine, he was in a severe car accident, suffering broken bones and permanent blindness. He literally could no longer escape his PTSD by leaving in a car or a boat. And his two support people died around the time of the accident. **"After they were both gone, I was kind of left out in the dark. So that's probably why I got help when I did, after the car accident."** Between the accident and the loss of his confidantes, James's symptoms worsened around 2008. He was formally diagnosed with PTSD around 2010.

To begin coping with his new life after the accident, James had to regain physical strength as well as learn to trust himself, now that he couldn't see. He did this through physical and occupational therapy, inpatient and outpatient talk therapy, and medication. He no longer needs the medication, as he's learned to manage the PTSD symptoms by reaching out to family or the Veterans Health Administration. He's also gained independence from his blindness with **"lots of devices that talk to me."**

Jean, age 73
"An avalanche of a grain of sand."

Jean is very open now about her depression, but she used to hide it from everyone. **"Always smiling and laughing to hide it,"** she says. Today, she says her mental illness can feel like **"an avalanche of a grain of sand."** But on good days between her episodes of depression, Jean says with a smile, **"Oh! This is how other people feel!"**

Jean never thought she'd live beyond age forty. She recalls her depressed feelings starting around age ten, and she wished to kill herself when she was young. It wasn't until age nineteen, during her nursing training, that she realized she had clinical depression.

Jean lives with recurrent depression (where episodes of depression are separated by usual functioning) with underlying dysthymia (a long-lasting mood disorder not as severe as major depression), anxiety, and posttraumatic stress disorder. She doesn't go into deep depression anymore, and electroconvulsive therapy took away most of her suicidal thoughts. But her depression can still be affected by stress related to her adult children's lives and her own health problems.

"A lot of people think that people with a mental illness are crazy or dangerous," she says. **"Maybe for the minority, often because they stopped taking their meds. Mental illness is a physical disease of the brain. A mental illness is invisible—looks normal but may have some odd behaviors."** With a chuckle, she adds, **"I might be crazy, but I'm not stupid."**

Jean's wonderful sense of humor and hearty laughter are apparent throughout the interview. She makes a point to discuss activities she really enjoys: meeting up with high school classmates, going to live theater, singing in her church, and writing poetry. Jean has a big heart too. **"Big enough to love everybody,"** »

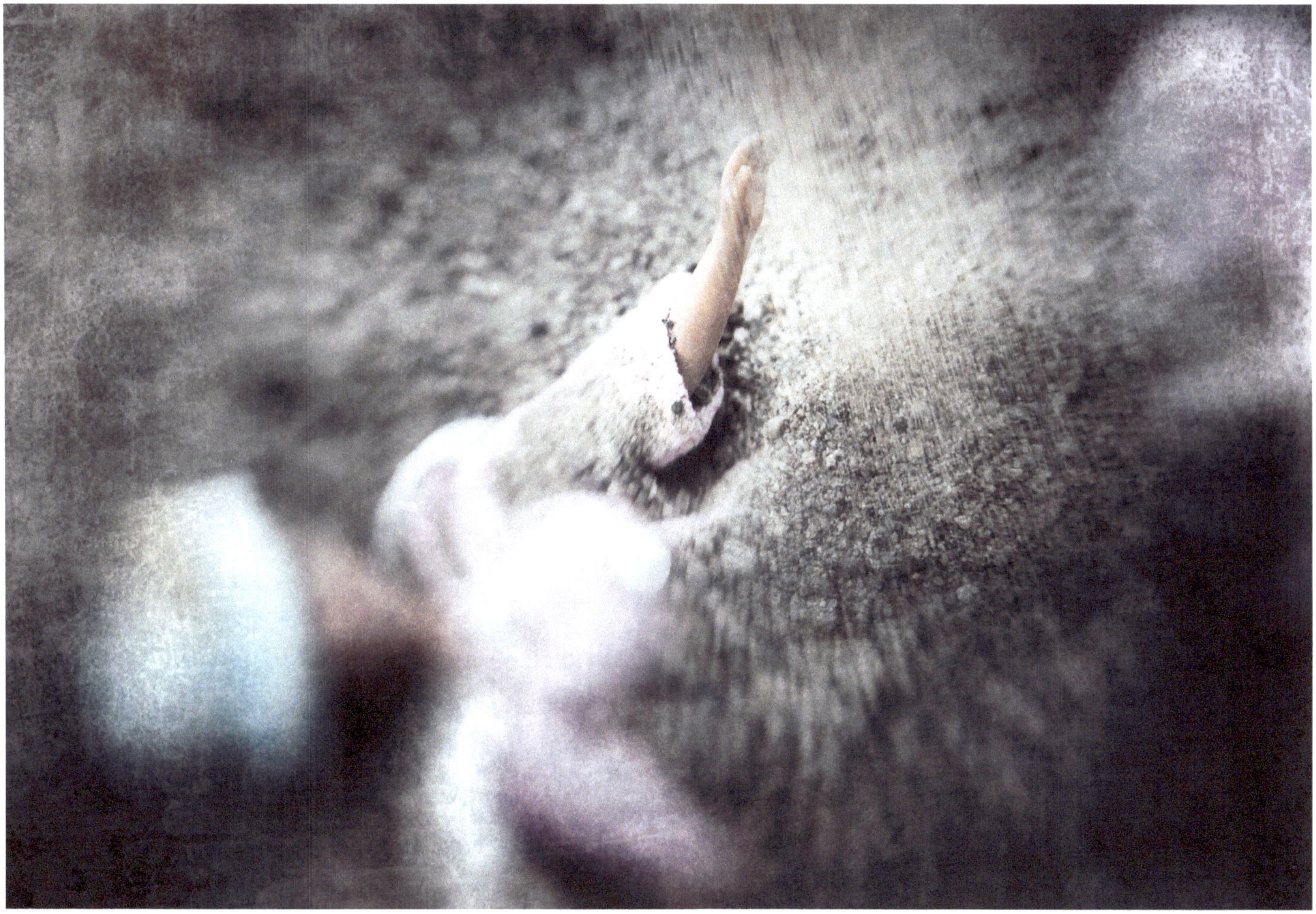

"An avalanche of a grain of sand."

she says. She shows some of that love by volunteering at a day care and in a special-education classroom. Her advice to others living with a mental illness: **"Don't go off your medication without your doctor's OK. I see a lot of people stop, with negative consequences."**

Jenna, age 26
"Constraint. Never going to let go."

Jenna wanted to be interviewed because she firmly believes in breaking down the stigma of mental illness. **"To do that, you have to talk about it,"** she says. **"Mental health is not a linear journey. Up and down, left and right. It's constantly changing. You have to be patient."**

Jenna's diagnosis includes posttraumatic stress disorder (PTSD) with major depression and generalized anxiety disorder. How does it feel? **"Constraint. Right next to me. Tight. Like it's never going to let go."** Her job and other distractions keep her going, but it's always a challenge. She continues to work through her feelings and is open to trying new therapies so she can eventually move on.

Jenna recalls feelings of depression as early as age twelve. That was when her parents discovered that her older brother had been sexually and physically abusing her for the last seven years. The abuse only ended when he moved out of the house a year earlier.

Her family reacted poorly to that discovery. Jenna says she experienced **"another five or so years of drama"** after that. She admits that she often feels mad about how her parents handled the situation when she was a teenager. She feels they were unsupportive. **"Are you lying?"** they'd ask her. They'd also tell her, **"Don't make me choose between my kids. You treat it like *I* did something wrong."**

Jenna struggles more with the aftermath of revealing the abuse than she does with the actual events of the abuse itself. **"During the experience, it was 'shut up, don't talk, move on.'"** She minimalized how she felt because she didn't want to upset her family even more. **"Friends and family act like you're a burden, and that is so traumatizing. I don't feel validated by the** »

"Constraint. Never going to let go."

people who are supposed to love me the most." To this day, she doesn't feel as though she gets real support from most of her family, other than her middle brother.

"It's on their terms."

By age sixteen, Jenna knew she needed help. She talked to her pediatrician, but she doesn't remember that » being helpful. So Jenna coped as best she could over those years. If she could go back in time, she'd advise young Jenna: **"If you want help, you can search for it yourself. You can do it. Your parents don't have to do it for you."**

Severe depression affected her in college and afterward. She remembers having suicidal thoughts early in college. **"But I just sucked it up and finished college."** Jenna also had suicidal thoughts at a time when she should have been celebrating. **"I had that moment before graduation of wanting to kill myself. Had the plan and suicide note for a month. But then decided not to. Don't know what changed my mind."** Even after college, Jenna didn't deal with work life very well. She struggled with feelings of **"I'm not enough."**

Not wanting to embarrass her mom if other people found out, Jenna didn't start therapy until age twenty-four. She credits therapy and being open about her situation for improving her life. For example, she learned how to think of a stop sign every time she has random, persistent thoughts of the past trauma and feelings of shame and failure. **"It's my fault"** or **"I'm not good enough,"** she sometimes tells herself. But visualizing the stop sign helps her prevent those thoughts from spiraling out of control and spilling into her work and relationships.

"Mental illness isn't your fault," she expresses. **"But it is your problem to work on. Put the time in. Try different therapists. Change meds if things aren't working. But you've got to do the work."** These are some of the lessons Jenna has learned about living with mental illness. **"It's a slow progression, and it's OK if that behavior doesn't change right now."**

Jenna wants people unfamiliar with PTSD to know it's complicated. **"Anyone can have it, not just POWs and soldiers in war. Trauma can come from anywhere."** She urges people to **"be open to listening. Don't write it off."**

And how does she as an adult now handle her mental illness and live a successful life? **"When I have bad days, it can be hard,"** she says. **"But I redefine what success looks like."**

Jenny, age 35

"Fear of being alone and abandoned."

Jenny is an engaging mosaic of a person—determined, sensitive, humorous, and caring. While she's fairly private about her mental illness, she wants to share her story so that **"everything I've been through is worth it."** Plus, she wants to help fight the stereotypes associated with mental illness. **"Just because I don't look depressed doesn't mean I'm not. I feel like my feelings are pushed aside because I'm nice and I smile."**

Jenny lives with depression, anxiety, and borderline personality disorder as well as a gambling addiction and eating disorder. **"I don't choose to feel this way. When you're depressed or suicidal, you believe it. I live with mental illness. Anybody can have it. It's not just a homeless person or someone in the military or abused. It can be a housewife, your teacher, your preacher. Anyone. Mental illness doesn't discriminate."**

At age fourteen, Jenny knew she needed help, but her struggles had gradually started a few years earlier. Moving to a new school at age twelve left her feeling very isolated. She had her first thoughts of suicide, and she began controlling her eating, including dabbling in bulimia. Over time, the suicidal thoughts and controlled eating worsened. By age fifteen, she had started cutting and hitting herself, followed by suicide attempts in high school and college. Her first hospitalization was for the eating disorder.

Jenny uses many concepts to describe what her mental illness feels like: **"Roller coaster. Exhausting. Fear of being alone and abandoned."** But she also feels **"more aware of the things around me and deeply empathic to the feelings of others around me."**

Residential treatment and working on coping skills in adult rehabilitation has helped Jenny a lot. With ongoing »

"Fear of being alone and abandoned."

therapy, a caseworker, and medication, she's better today at managing and recognizing her warning signs of depression. She'll enter partial hospitalization (a daytime intense-treatment setting) when she's having suicidal thoughts. But she's the first to point out that **"you're never cured. You just hope to manage things better."** Her last suicide attempt was over three years ago.

Her life today is a mixture of good and bad. She has a degree and her own business, but she frustratingly asks, **"Why isn't anything different?"** In her twenties, she wanted marriage and kids, but she feels that dream is lost now.

"Mental illness isn't easy," she expresses. **"It isn't curable, but it can be manageable. It's important to stay in therapy and take medication. Find a purpose, any purpose—it's what keeps you going."**

Joel, age 51
"Happy-go-lucky."

Today, Joel's schizoaffective disorder is well managed. A low-level headache, a side effect of a medication to help treat his disorder, is all he notices when he's still and quiet. His experience was more symptomatic between 1988 and 1998.

Joel was a young man of about twenty when his unmanaged mental illness forced him to start giving up a lot of his favorite activities. He let his hair and beard grow long, he smoked, he stayed up all night, and he drank a lot of coffee and strong tea. Sometimes he slept in a chair in a closet, cigarette dangling between his fingers, ashes falling to the floor.

Joel would sometimes hear auditory hallucinations that made negative comments. One such comment told him that friends and strangers knew every single one of his faults. He also had delusions, leading him to believe he was famous or that he had caused a superstorm the summer of 1987.

It didn't occur to Joel that his thoughts were delusional. Fortunately, his parents recognized that something was wrong. They admitted him into a treatment center where he received medication and was diagnosed with schizophrenia. His parents were always very supportive of him. In fact, Joel feels that **"when you have a good childhood, it cushions everything."**

After a medication change in 1998, Joel's life improved. There was a drastic reduction in his delusions, his hallucinations, and the physical pain of his past. Now he feels **"happy-go-lucky most of the time, like a sunny day with soft clouds."** He's been married since 2012 and is very active—mentoring, facilitating mental health groups, playing keyboard and coronet, singing, and volunteering. »

"Happy-go-lucky."

Joel understands there are many obstacles to navigating mental illness. He believes there are **"not enough doctors or support, and the stigma is still bad."** He also feels that TV shows perpetuate the misconception that mental illness results in violence. (Note: According to the 2016 *Gun Violence and Mental Illness* study by Lisa H. Gold and Robert I. Simon of Georgetown University, only 3 percent of all violent crimes are linked to severe mental illness.)

To others living with mental illness, Joel encourages you to **"hang in there. Most likely it will get better. Everything mellows out as you get older."** ❊

John, age 70

"Black. Down a tunnel with no light . . ."

John lives with major depression. He deals with it quietly, often shutting himself in. On good days, he feels alive, with the energy to do everyday things rather than just sit. But on bad days, the depression weighs him down. **"Depression sucks,"** he says. **"Zaps the life out of you."** He describes his depression as **"the color black, going down a tunnel with no light at the end, knowing that a train is coming to hit me."**

He's quick to admit responsibility for where he's at today, both financially and emotionally. And that leads to his advice to other people: **"If you find yourself in a bad [relationship] situation, don't stay. It won't help. Make sure you're happy."** John believes that if he'd gotten out of his prior marriage sooner, he'd be better emotionally today. **"But then I wouldn't have met my current wife,"** he adds as a warm smile crosses his face. She's the love of his life.

John copes with his depression in several ways. He has two dogs, which comfort him with love and calm when he's not feeling well. During the interview, the dogs cuddle in his lap. Having made eight or nine suicide attempts, John feels the suicide crisis line has been crucial to his survival many times. Therapy, cooking, and baking have helped him move forward. In addition, journaling has had a big positive impact on his life, as has his faith.

John shares one of the biggest misconceptions about mental illness: **"We're not a danger to you. We're just trying to do our best to get through and not have meltdowns."**

Being part of this book **"allowed me to feel good about something other than my issues. Maybe I will be able to help someone else understand and realize just how debilitating depression really is to the person dealing with it."**

"Black. Down a tunnel with no light . . ."

Karen, age 44
"Confusing."

For Karen, living with mental illness is a constant struggle. She's been diagnosed with paranoid schizophrenia, anxiety, a depressive disorder, and obsessive-compulsive disorder with hoarding. She describes her mental illness as feeling like **"a constant problem. I can't help the way I feel, and that's confusing."**

Karen struggled with hoarding in her teens. It got to the point where her parents would throw away the unmanageable piles of completed schoolwork when she wasn't home. In her early twenties, she started hearing voices that **"sounded like the devil saying negative things about God."**

Life is better today but is still filled with ups and downs. She sees a counselor and does better when she takes her medication. That said, Karen admits to being inconsistent with her medication because of the side effects. And she still struggles a lot with paranoia at her job.

She wishes she would have heard this when she was young, and Karen also wants others to know **"that you're a capable person that can get through life**." Karen offers encouragement to **"get help—you don't want stuff bottled up inside you."** ✖

"Confusing."

Kelly, age 28
"Frenzied energy inside me."

"One of the hardest things about mental illness," Kelly says, "is feeling like everything you've done is wrong, when you just want to be accepted and understood."

While Kelly is willing to talk about her depression and anxiety, talking too much about it brings her down, especially if she feels it's bringing others down as well. Kelly explains how she reached this conclusion: "The less I felt understood, the more I needed to talk about it, but the worse I felt. That was when I realized that people don't need to understand. Only I need to be OK with how I feel."

Kelly tries to find the humor as she reflects on her experience. Lightheartedly, she says she's had anxiety since birth. "But it has been for as long as I can remember," she adds. The anxiety is a struggle. "It's like bees in my head. Frenzied energy inside me."

In her darkest moments with depression, which began in her teens, she felt "really calm and quiet, my brain shutting down and not feeling anything. The way down to the bottom was sharp and painful because I'd fight it." She never had suicidal thoughts, however. "There was always this logical part of my brain. I never crossed that line of wanting to kill myself. My anxiety and fear of dying prevented me from crossing the line."

Kelly reached a turning point at seventeen, when she felt she was falling apart and not handling life well. She went to a doctor, who prescribed antidepressants. But because the doctor didn't provide other alternatives, Kelly didn't feel personally committed to the antidepressants. "I didn't feel like it was my choice to start taking them," she says. So she intentionally stopped taking them after a short time. "I'm stubborn and wanted to figure out what the actual problem »

"Frenzied energy inside me."

was with my body, not just treat the symptoms,"** she explains. She knew the root cause of her depression, and she believed healing those wounds would benefit her more. She sums up her overarching belief: **"I never believed I was inherently broken."** As she reflects on her depression, she says, **"I always had this sureness that I'd »** beat it—the depression wasn't going to be a dark cloud anymore."

To improve her mental health, she tried therapy. She admits to not being ready for it, though, so she didn't feel it helped. Instead, she proactively researched different prayer practices, such as meditation. Those resonated with her. In addition, she began avoiding toxic situations and learned to become more introspective. And she learned to stop ruminating. **"I've worked hard at becoming mindful of my thought patterns, stopping them in their tracks before they become too out of control."**

What has also helped over time is thinking happier thoughts and writing lists of things she's grateful for. Yet when others had told her to do this in the past, she didn't want to hear it, so she fought the idea. She believes she had to discover these methods herself.

"Overall, life is much easier now than years ago," she states. **"I rewired my brain, so to speak. All the self-sabotaging behaviors—I've pulled them apart. Threw them away. No meds. No therapy."** She also credits **"having people in my life willing to put up** with me being a work in progress for a while."

Kelly is an artist, and learning to deal with anxiety and depression has affected her art in positive ways. **"It has made it so much easier to create, because I'm coming from a place of confidence and comfort. I'm actually more creative now."**

The main thing Kelly wants you to understand about mental illness is, **"Our culture needs to be more accepting of needing help. Flaws are not a weakness. Mental illness is a public concern, but we're all on our own personal journey and need to support each other on that journey."** She continues that thought by adding, **"When you have someone with mental illness around you, you need to let them know you care. That it's not a flaw—it's an illness."**

Kelly's quick to point out that her path is one of many ways to live successfully with mental illness and work toward improved mental health. **"It can get better. Whatever options you choose—therapy, medication, mindfulness, spirituality—it doesn't have to be painful all the time."** 🞂

Kerstin, age 18
"Empowered."

"I want an explanation why I feel how I do. But I don't always have one. Sometimes I just need to cry."

Kerstin knows how difficult it can be to express your feelings when you don't know why you feel them. **"People in your life need to have a lot of patience,"** she says. **"You can be doing well all day, come home, and suddenly begin crying for no apparent reason."**

Kerstin lives with depression and anxiety. She says it's hard to put depression into words. **"There are so many different ways to feel it. So many symptoms and 'whys.'"** To help describe depression, Kerstin uses the idea of a lamp. **"The base of the lamp represents my family and friends—always there supporting me. And the light switch is the depression. Turn it on, and the future looks bright. Turn it off, and it's darkness."**

She was often described as a "nervous Nellie" when she was young. She remembers a stressful, worried experience in kindergarten when her mom didn't pick her up on time, due to a miscommunication. At age thirteen, she was diagnosed with depression after what she describes as **"feeling extra sad."**

At its worst, her depression resulted in self-harm (such as cutting herself and taking burning-hot showers) along with suicidal thoughts and attempts. She was secretive about her feelings. **"I thought I had power over it by doing the self-harming behaviors,"** she says. **"Looking back, I can tell it was a cry for help."** Kerstin was admitted to a crisis center and inpatient treatment a couple of times when her symptoms became extreme.

Family, close friends, therapy, and medication have been important in managing her symptoms. Two coping techniques are also helpful when she's feeling sad: cleaning and grocery shopping. Kerstin views cleaning and » rearranging the furniture as symbolic of a new beginning. Even grocery shopping is a reminder about control and the future. Knowing she'll be making a meal helps push her to feel happier.

Feelings of hopelessness ebb and flow for her. Sometimes they're driven by life events, such as breaking up with a boyfriend, high school graduation, and going to college. Depression can feed the anxiety, fueling the worry and hopelessness.

Despite the sadness she's experienced in the past and present, Kerstin is really happy with where she's at right now. **"I feel empowered that I made it through the bad times,"** she says, **"despite how hard the battle was to get past feeling like the world would end."** She adds, **"Life feels like it's worth living now. I wouldn't change my past, because I am more open to other people and their emotions now."**

She recently got a tattoo that says WARR;OR. The semicolon is a symbol of solidarity and hope for people struggling with suicide, depression, and other mental illness. "A semicolon is used when an author could have chosen to end their sentence, but chose not to. The author is you, and the sentence is your life," explains Project Semicolon's website.

Her advice to everyone: **"Other people struggle with depression, but we experience it differently. Take the time to understand what someone else is feeling. Listen. Help each other."** ✠

"Empowered."

Kirk, age 48
"Stranded, lost, alone, and confused."

"I'm no different," Kirk says. **"It can happen to anybody. It's not always easy to see somebody with mental illness. It can be invisible, almost a hidden disease."** Kirk is a quiet man, an observer, a thinker— but he's also positive about life. He's mentored another person living with mental illness, he plans to get his GED, and he's learning to play the harmonica.

Kirk lives with posttraumatic stress disorder, depression, psychosis (which he describes as sometimes seeing and hearing things that aren't real), anxiety, and a short-term-memory learning disability. He guesses he was about eight years old when his mental illness began. He remembers his dad intentionally pouring a pot of hot coffee over him. His dad was often absent, being away in the military. Kirk's brothers abused him both physically (beating him severely) and emotionally. They forced him to drink alcohol, and they forced him to do cocaine and use pot by age eight, which eventually led to addiction.

Even outside of his home life, his grade school years were rough—his family moved frequently, leaving him with few friends. He was bullied by fellow students. Yet Kirk did his share of fighting back to survive.

In seventh grade, Kirk recognized something wasn't right emotionally. This was the first time he tried to kill himself. His depression hit him hard when his dad died at sixteen. Kirk left home. Permanently.

During his adult years, Kirk attempted suicide a few times. He also almost died after drinking alcohol and smoking pot to such excess that he went into convulsions and stopped breathing. If his buddy hadn't revived him, Kirk wouldn't have lived.

At age forty, Kirk voluntarily sought treatment for his addictions because of this experience. It was also the first time he got help with his mental illness. He found »

"Stranded, lost, alone, and confused."

additional therapy in a group home setting. He just wanted a better life.

Looking back, Kirk recalls a time when he'd hitchhike in the desert and not get picked up—a real-life metaphor for his occasional feelings of being **"stranded, lost, alone, and confused."** Even though his life today can still be difficult, it's better than he thought it would be. He honestly thought he'd be dead by now.

"Don't give up. You're not alone," he tells others with mental illness. To people who don't live with mental illness, he says, **"I'm no different than you are. I just have a few more issues. Sometimes you don't know you have problems, too, because you don't notice."** He added, **"And it's not contagious."**

Linda, age 63
"Bounce from task to task"

"If you learn someone has a mental illness," Linda explains, **"try not to make assumptions based on their diagnosis. Even if you know what the diagnosis is, that doesn't mean you've walked in their shoes. Just ask them to explain what it feels like to them."** Linda expands on this by saying, **"Remember that not everyone experiences it the same way. Each [diagnosis] is a broad category, with many variations of severity of symptoms. And maybe you don't need medication— just ways to learn how to deal with it."**

Linda's bipolar depression and seasonal affective disorder began gradually in her teens, and it became noticeable around the age of nineteen. Initially, her depression was only an issue during fall and winter. She dealt with it by spending time outside in the sun and by using light therapy indoors. By her late twenties, however, that wasn't enough to manage the symptoms. The depression had become more than seasonal, leading to a diagnosis of bipolar depression.

In the beginning, Linda didn't take any medication; she didn't want to. And so her moods would swing. Sometimes she'd feel as if she had all the energy in the world. **"Everything seemed just fine, even when it wasn't, because I'd bounce from task to task."** Other times, she'd feel as if **"all my energy was gone, sucked into a black hole that felt like it would last indefi-**nitely." During this time prior to starting medication, she was suicidal.

Linda's turning point came during a hospitalization after a suicide attempt. She met a staff person who told her that she herself had bipolar and took medication. **"I was shocked!"** Linda recalls. **"I couldn't tell [she had bipolar depression]. She had a job, was married, and was fine! She was a positive role model for me. I was so worried about being able to parent. But she made me think 'I can live through this *and* live a normal life.'"**

Inspired by that conversation, Linda agreed to take medication. **"It was a daunting possibility to take medication forever,"** she admits, **"but my husband convinced me it wasn't the worst thing."** It took a few different medications, but she did find one that worked best. **"Everything sort of evened out,"** she says. **"I regained some cautious optimism about my prospects for a decent life as a mother and spouse, and I was able to hold down a full-time job again."**

Through it all, Linda completed college as well as balanced her life as a wife and mother. Family was always a great support system for her. However, she remained secretive about her illness in her work environment. **"No one knew because 'you just don't talk about it.' I thought people's perceptions of me would be »** negatively affected if they knew. **They might doubt my abilities.”**

Talk therapy was most helpful during Linda's worst years, but medication has been the common thread throughout her life to manage her symptoms. Now in her sixties, Linda says life has been much easier the past ten years. Even during the chaos of her husband dying, she realized her coping skills were much better.

If you're struggling with your diagnosis or suspect you need help, Linda urges, **“Don't wait so long to get help, even though you have periods where things are just fine. It can be managed. It's not the overall determining factor in your life. So many medications are available now compared to twenty or thirty years ago. It might feel unmanageable in the beginning, but it doesn't have to be.”** ✠

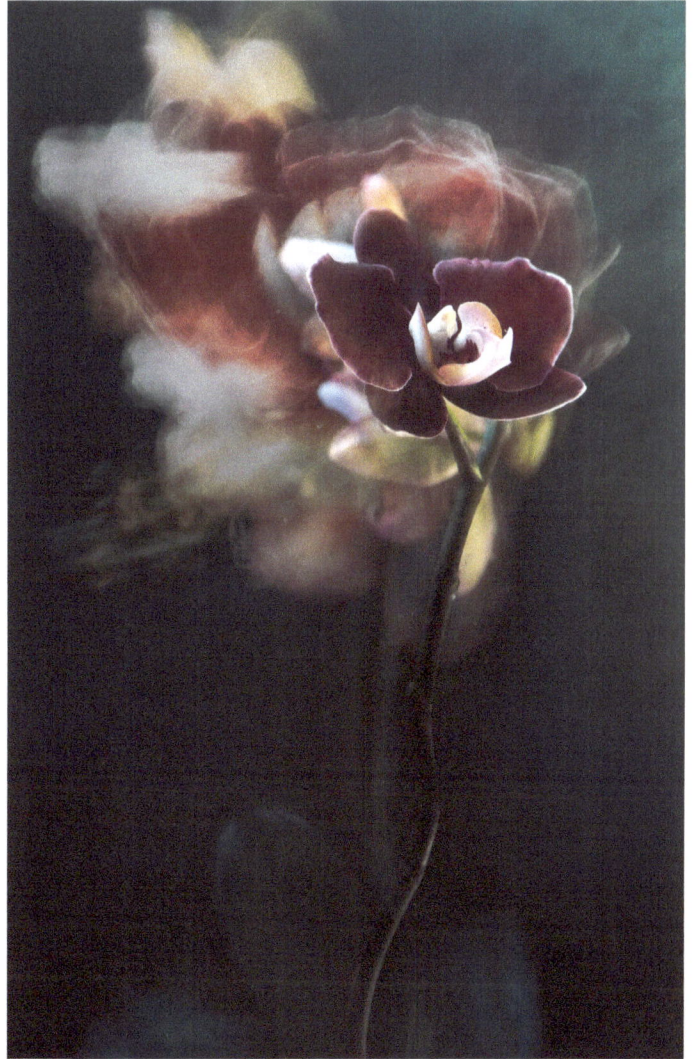

“Bounce from task to task”

"Lyla," age 57

"Trapped. Lonely. Frightened. Frustrated."

You know when you meet someone and you can't help but return a smile? That's Lyla. She's one of those people you like in an instant. Her shy smile is endearing. And she has a lot to say when someone takes the time to listen.

Lyla lives with schizoaffective disorder, which for her includes paranoia, depression, and anxiety—the more paranoia she feels, the worse her anxiety. She also lives with borderline intellectual functioning, which can make it difficult for her to learn and understand other people.

"I wish people would understand that it's hard for me to understand words," she says. **"I'm not like they are. Some think that I should be like them, and I'm not. Take the time to let me explain. It's hard for me to get words out quickly. Be patient with me."** Lyla feels this is the hardest thing to make others understand. She says that when people are impatient and try to rush her, it just makes things worse.

Lyla's schizoaffective disorder started as a child, but she didn't receive help until she was about twenty. She recalls, **"I would keep quiet about bad dreams about my family, even though they were good to me. I'd just cry. I didn't want anyone to feel it was their fault."** While her family was supportive, she's not sure her teachers understood what was happening. Lyla felt so alone in school, unable to ask for help or express her inner feelings. Today, she can look back and explain that she felt **"trapped. Lonely. Frightened. Frustrated."**

As an adult, Lyla has faced and still faces challenges. During one low point, she didn't eat or bathe. She was confused and crying constantly, unable to put thoughts into words. Her symptoms were severe enough to result in her being hospitalized and receiving electroconvulsive therapy. »

"Trapped. Lonely. Frightened. Frustrated."

Even today, her dreams can get really confusing, as it's difficult for her to separate them from reality. If Lyla is having a good day, she has only a few bad dreams; sometimes she has none at all. But when her paranoia and anxiety increase, it comes out in her dreams. She recounts past dreams where **"the walls were caving in and I couldn't get out. Everything was coming down on me."**

While life today is still a struggle for Lyla, it's better than it used to be. She hopes others **"know that there is support out there and to not be afraid to ask for it. It will help you in the long run. It did me."** Lyla feels her therapists support her by encouraging her to pursue things she can do. **"They have faith in my potential."**

Mark, age 57
"Incomplete."

Mark is very thoughtful during the interview, taking time to really think about the questions. What can his mental illness feel like to him? **"Sometimes it feels like I have a different face,"** he replies. **"An average person's face, but partially faded. Incomplete. Kind of like I'm half-invisible, off in the corner of a room, ghostly and distorted."**

Mark's experience with mild depression and anxiety are due in large part to contracting encephalitis as a baby. The resulting brain injury caused slower physical development and possibly cognitive changes that left him more vulnerable to depression.

Mark was in his late thirties when several people close to him died in a short period. This is when he reached out for the first time. **"I just knew I needed some form of help,"** he says. He went through a series of counselors before he found one he liked. **"Try to get the courage to ask for the help you need—and the right kind,"** he

encourages others. **"Don't accept the first type of help if it's not working."**

When Mark was at his lowest point emotionally, he drank too much alcohol, which negatively affected not only his mood but also his ability to hold down a job. He felt alone, with no one to talk to. He briefly thought about suicide but never attempted it.

What did Mark do for a better life? He stopped drinking over fifteen years ago. In addition, Mark has gone to counseling off and on over the years, and medication has helped too. While some parts of his life have improved over time, diabetic nerve pain frustrates and brings him down the most today.

To those wishing to understand mental illness, Mark says, **"Try to understand the individual first. Don't define them by their problems. Each person's life is equal. Nobody's more important than the other."** ✠

"Meredith," age 18
"It's always there."

"It's always there."

Bright, vibrant, and wise beyond her years, Meredith has lived with depression, anxiety, and attention-deficit/hyperactivity disorder (ADHD). She's also diagnosed with body dysmorphic disorder, which includes an eating disorder. Most of the conversation during the interview centers around this.

While they're easier to manage now than in the past, Meredith still deals with worrisome thoughts about her weight. The intensity of these thoughts varies, depending upon how much sleep she gets or how much stress she's under. Meeting a new person often triggers a lot of negative thoughts—worries and assumptions that this new person thinks the worst about her. At one time, Meredith was also hyperaware of people listening to her chew. The smile in her voice is obvious when she says, **"I'm glad that's subsided."**

Her mental health journey began in Colombia, where she was born. Neglected at birth, she suffered from malnourishment. She was adopted at age two by a family in the United States. Meredith believes that the malnourishment became the foundation for the body dysmorphia and eating disorder, despite the fact that she had access to plenty of healthy food after being adopted.

For her ADHD diagnosis, Meredith recalls not being able to stay seated in kindergarten, though she grew out of it over the years. Her depression and anxiety started around age twelve, but she wasn't formally diagnosed until about two years later. Most of her friends and classmates lacked understanding, thinking she was faking it for attention.

Meredith attempted to kill herself multiple times. An overdose was finally the wake-up call Meredith's mother needed to realize her daughter's feelings were real. »

Meredith's dad was quiet about everything but not in denial. Most importantly, she felt treated fairly and loved.

During this time, Meredith went to treatment for drug abuse and depression. She became sober, but she ended up trading one addiction for another—drugs for an eating disorder. She felt disgusted when looking at her body, and she obsessively weighed herself over thirty times a day. She kept this secret from her friends and family and would dismiss them if they showed concern over her weight loss. For her, it was a game to control what she ate or didn't eat, and that was all that mattered. She saw it as having the power to act on her desire to look like a model. Meredith feels there's a lot of stigma around needing to be a certain weight to fit in, and it affects both women and men.

Her boyfriend was supportive and influential in her getting help for the eating disorder. She was in treatment for the majority of high school. Meredith credits Alcoholics Anonymous, Narcotics Anonymous, and Eating Disorders Anonymous as being incredibly helpful. She found inspiration in hearing people's stories and seeing them healthy.

For people reading this who have an eating disorder, Meredith wants you to know it gets easier. She was honest, though: **"It gets worse before it gets better. But there are others out there like you, and you can just let go and get help. The struggle is real. And if you have to make a sacrifice to get yourself help, it's worth it."**

Meredith really thought she'd die before age sixteen. **"Today, I'm not as sad. I'm determined and hopeful because my life is getting better. I love who I am today. Because of my own experiences, I'm open minded and feel like I can connect with anyone."** ✠

"It's always there."

Mickey, age 61
"Like a lead blanket."

With the strength Mickey has now, she wishes she could have told her teenage self, **"You're a good person. You deserve to be treated with kindness and respect. To be loved. To feel happiness and joy."**

Despite waves of adversity throughout her life, Mickey remains quietly strong and defiant. She manages posttraumatic stress disorder (PTSD), anxiety, and depression. For people unfamiliar with mental illness, she wants you to understand, **"We're normal people like everyone else. We laugh, love, go to work. There are a lot of people with mental illness who function just fine."**

Mickey experienced feelings of depression after giving birth to her son when she was a teenager, but she didn't seek help. A few years later, Mickey's husband died. At that point, she visited a therapist—only to be dismissed with the comment, **"You're fine."** But Mickey knew she wasn't fine, so she went to a second doctor, who diagnosed her with chronic and severe depression. After being prescribed helpful medication, Mickey realized what it meant to feel OK after years of feeling depressed. **"I was depressed back when I was a kid,"** she realizes. **"But at the time, it felt normal."**

In Mickey's midtwenties, she experienced a low point in her life due to a severe depressive episode. She considered suicide at her darkest moment. She remembers how **"it feels like a cold, dark place. The depression feels big and heavy, like a lead blanket."** She was hospitalized for a month. In the past, she had kept her mental illness a secret from everyone but immediate family and a few friends. This time was different. More people discovered her situation. Many friendships disappeared, and acquaintances acted as if they didn't know her.

Mickey regrets not sharing more of her feelings »

sooner with her dad. Her father never really understood her mental illness. He thought it was **"like getting chicken pox—once treated, it doesn't return."** The last few years of his life, she shared more detail about her experiences, and that was integral to him understanding his daughter a little better.

Her father wasn't the only one who struggled to understand mental illness. **"Even today, I know people who think it should just go away after a little medication and treatment."** She remarks how **"a psychiatrist once told me to 'just accept' that my medication wasn't helping."** Not willing to be defeated, Mickey found a new psychiatrist, who tried different things. It resulted in a better emotional outcome.

Symptoms of her mental illness are better controlled now. She can recognize flare-ups and try to deal with them sooner. Even so, depression and the intermittent feelings of worthlessness are the most challenging for Mickey. And sometimes PTSD can exacerbate her depression. Mickey attempts to reverse that downward spiral and avoid that cold, dark place with **"proper ongoing care, counseling, prescribed medication, knowing my signs of when I'm going downhill, then having a plan to help what to do."** She adds, **"Without medication and lots of therapy, I wouldn't be here today."**

Mickey admits her life isn't what she expected it would be when she was young. Physical and mental health problems have held her back. She herself believed the stigma about people with mental illness; she never finished college because she thought she wasn't good enough to get a degree. Financially, she didn't make enough for a comfortable home and a good, reliable car. Dreams of travel are still just that, dreams.

However, Mickey's present life is also better than she could have imagined. She has happiness and joy. She has the love of family and friends and a dog she adores. She has her job as a childcare provider, and she's continued to educate herself. Plus, Mickey knows she's made a difference in people's lives by being a grandma, by being a positive influence as a paraprofessional and childcare provider, and by being an advocate and resource for those with mental illness. Of paramount importance is her role as parent. With heartfelt emotion, choking back tears, she says, **"Being a good mom was the most important thing I've done in my life."**

Paula, age 63
"Strange and scary, like I don't have control."

Paula has a sparkle about her when she talks and smiles. And yet she says about her past, **"I felt I deserved the pain."**

After suffering emotional, sexual, and physical abuse throughout her childhood and teens, Paula became a cutter, which lasted decades. She's been diagnosed with depression and borderline personality disorder. Earlier in her life, she was misdiagnosed with schizophrenia. Dating back to her early teens, she has been hospitalized many times for suicide attempts or depression. She has used alcohol to cope throughout most of her life. She even gave up her children, fearing she'd begin abusing them as her mother abused her. Paula trusted the men she dated, but they would start abusing her. **"I believed I deserved to be abused."**

Paula describes her mental illness as sometimes feeling **"strange and scary, like I don't have control. The negative thoughts about myself—I really take them to heart."** Her suicidal thoughts and negative self-image used to be much worse, though they're still present. **"Do my suicidal thoughts go away? No, but they aren't as dominant. I thought I'd [always] be the 'Paula with depression,' but I know how to help fight it now."** On a good day, though, these thoughts aren't as strong. **"I can finally have a good day, a happy day!"** she says. **"I feel like crafting, making dishcloths, and listening to calming meditation."**

In her fifties, Paula received a large influx of emotional support. She got a job, and she found her therapist and support groups to be very empowering. **"The support groups have made me stronger. I'm around people who are happy and who support me."** She also says the support from police and hospital staff are so much better now than in the past. »

"Strange and scary, like I don't have control."

"I went through the abuse," Paula states, **"but I know I don't have to focus on it. I like myself today. I used to always put myself down. Today I know I have support. And there's hope, and I can build myself up."**

If you're struggling, Paula says, **"hang in there. There's hope for you, and there is support available to you."**

Richard, age 65
"Red for love and anger."

"Treat me as a person, not as an illness or diagnosis. Someone who loves and has loved, not a sick person. *See beyond the illness.*"

Richard was thirty years old, married, and fresh out of graduate school when his life took an unexpected path. He had what was then called a psychotic break. He began mishearing and misinterpreting sounds. For instance, he thought the sound of the refrigerator running meant something. Other times, he wouldn't hear the actual words someone had spoken to him. Instead, he'd hear other words entirely. Sometimes Richard's misinterpretations were positive; on a bad day, negative.

He was eventually diagnosed with schizoaffective disorder with bipolar disorder. Day treatment was very helpful early on, in addition to medication, which he still takes regularly.

Today, at times, he still struggles. The delusions are frustrating. They are real to him. His mental illness feels like **"the color red. Red for love. And red for anger."** The reality is, life with mental illness isn't easy. Over the years, he's had many suicidal thoughts. He came close twice but never actually attempted it. **"Resignedly, I'm not going to die,"** he says.

When he was younger, some friends and family were embarrassed by Richard's mental illness, causing him shame, sadness, and low self-esteem. Over the years, however, he's been open about his illness, which has saved many friendships and relationships.

Monica, his wife of over forty years, was honest about the effect Richard's mental illness had on their relationship. **"It's been very difficult. We were even separated for a year. But Richard's good days can be so good—the Richard I fell in love with."** »

"Red for love and anger."

Richard has a message to people trying to navigate relationships while living with a mental illness: **"Surviving as a married person is possible. A family, a child—you can flourish and cope. Life is not all misery. You can love people and be loved."**

For those without mental illness, Richard hopes you can admire those who have survived and coped and that you can identify in some small way. **"We are survivors. We are the people dressed in white who have gone through the period of trial."**

Monica adds, **"I wish people would understand. If someone has a cancer diagnosis, they get support from everyone. People don't understand the respect that someone should get for enduring this."**

Richard echoes her statement: **"The stigma is still so real. We're just people with an illness. We often feel so worthless, and that's why it's doubly important that mental illness is understood."** ❈

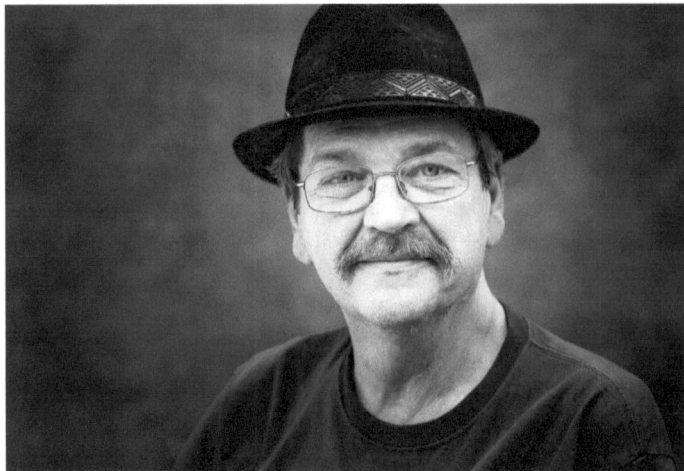

Sloan, age 62
"A suffocating, warm, fuzzy blanket."

"Strange, the things that bring you back," Sloan says. **"One time a guy who looked just like my son asked if I needed help. I was standing on the side of the road on a bridge near my car. I said I was okay and made up some excuse about the engine overheating. He said, 'Have a nice day.' That was enough to stop me."** That suicide attempt was a symptom of Sloan's severe depression. He also lives with attention-deficit/hyperactivity disorder (ADHD), bipolar II disorder, and borderline personality disorder.

Sloan's mental illness wasn't diagnosed until he was forty-eight years old. When he thinks back, though, he knows it started in his teens. **"You just think you're like everyone else, so you don't ask for help,"** he says of his younger years.

The final straw came in 2004. While Sloan was in the middle of other personal turmoil, his wife asked for a divorce. Overwhelmed, Sloan made his first suicide attempt. This is also when he started getting professional help.

With multiple diagnoses, each aspect of Sloan's mental illness feels different. For instance, his ADHD symptoms are **"frustrating."** It can be very difficult to accomplish any one thing. **"It's like procrastination on steroids sometimes,"** he explains. When it comes to his borderline personality disorder, the symptom he fights the most is feeling **"entitled."** He constantly checks himself and has learned habits that help counteract that feeling.

Bipolar II is marked by cycles of depression and hypomania. Hypomania is an elevated state, though it's less intense than mania. Sloan says his hypomania feels **"AWESOME!"** He becomes very focused with high energy. He describes it as feeling **"like being well rested with two cups of coffee."** But when he's severely » depressed, **"it can feel like a suffocating, warm, fuzzy blanket."**

Both his bipolar II disorder and borderline personality disorder have unpredictable cycles that can last hours or days. Sometimes he'll have normal sleep cycles. Other times, he'll sleep for twenty hours, then be awake for thirty hours straight. This makes it impossible to hold a traditional nine-to-five job.

Through it all, Sloan is multitalented, having learned several careers (electrician, plumber, and programmer) and art forms (painting, poetry, photography, and wood carving). He uses his art to help manage his mental illness. Anything creative helps him get into his head and **"dig into the dusty bins,"** as he calls them.

In addition to therapy and medication, other tools in his illness management toolbox include meditation and a unique method of creating a rhyming poem literally one step and one word at a time while out for a walk. Sloan also works hard at recognizing the limitations of black-and-white thinking. For instance, if he sees only one or two answers to a problem, he'll ask someone else for advice, knowing there might be more solutions. Sloan uses all these tools when dealing with his various triggers. **"Figuring out which tool to use takes practice,"** he adds with a grin.

Sloan admits he still struggles with his mental illness. **"But it's not a blind struggle anymore,"** he says. To explain, he uses the analogy of finding yourself in a lake. **"A blind struggle is when you don't know how to swim and can't get out. Knowing how to swim and being able to get out is better."**

Sloan uses another analogy to describe how frustrating it can be to get treatment for mental illness. **"Imagine this: you break your leg, go to the emergency room, and you get an X-ray and a cast. Now imagine if your broken leg were treated like a mental illness. 'Here's an X-ray machine, some developer, and instructions on how to set your leg. Now you do it yourself.'"**

If you have a mental illness or suspect something isn't quite right, Sloan encourages you to get the help you need. **"Choosing a therapist isn't as simple as finding a doctor to fix a broken leg. There are a lot of therapists who won't be the right match for you. If it's a bad experience, don't give up! You won't hurt their feelings. Find a new one that you're comfortable with."**

Sloan also urges you to look past the labels from the *Diagnostic and Statistical Manual of Mental Disorders*, the manual used by mental health professionals. **"They are just that—labels. Labels only define symptoms. But they don't define *who* or *what* you are!"**

Sloan is a firm believer in being open and honest with others about his mental illness. In fact, his openness inspired some family members, including Sloan's son, to seek therapy themselves.

Sloan, like many others, is fighting to reduce the stigma and discrimination of mental illness. **"The worst part of stigma is the stigma we have ourselves. It prevents us from getting treatment."** He adds, **"People who are diagnosed and in treatment are stronger than your average person. It takes a lot of strength to admit you have a mental illness—and even more to get help."** ✖

Susan, age 62
"Trapped and flawed."

"I'm not a diagnosis; I'm a person," Susan states. Despite struggling with her own feelings about her mental illness, she is very much an advocate for decreasing the discrimination often associated with it. **"There are millions of people with mental illness, and it's nothing to be afraid of."**

When talking to Susan, one is struck by her wonderful mix of strength and vulnerability, combined with a fantastic sense of humor. She was diagnosed only a couple of years ago with major depression and anxiety. Looking back, Susan feels she's lived with moderate depression most of her life. Then when her husband died four years ago, her symptoms became worse. She's also addicted to alcohol and pain medication.

Susan admits it's hard to talk about her depression and anxiety, whereas she's more comfortable speaking about her addictions. That's because she struggles with shame when it comes to her depression and anxiety. When she was diagnosed, her family reacted with anger, denial, and misunderstanding. Her parents refused to recognize that she had depression. Susan tried to ignore their reactions, but the history of blame in her family triggered her to place the blame on herself.

Susan describes her anxiety, depression, and chemical dependency as **"feeling trapped in a flawed body."** She's learning to accept the diagnosis and trying to let go of the resentment and anger. **"I don't want to be angry anymore."**

Susan's day-to-day life is still a struggle—**"a work in progress,"** she says. Through therapy, she's learned techniques (which she calls her **"fanny pack"**) to deal with life's stressors.

To those who live with mental illness, Susan wants you to know, **"There's hope. You *can* do this!"** ✠

"Trapped and flawed."

Tabara, age 15
"Empty. Drowning."

Tabara is an intelligent, insightful, and tenacious teenager who wants to go to college and help others living with mental illness. She's already having an impact by sharing her personal experience.

Tabara copes with depression and anxiety today but was diagnosed with emotional and behavioral disorders when she was younger. **"The intensity of feelings is hard to describe,"** she says. **"Being anxious and feeling everything is ending. Or being so sad I can't get out of bed. Like I'm fine one second, and then it will smack me, and I'm drowning. For days, weeks, then it's gone. Then when I'm not in a funk, it feels miles away."**

Tabara's symptoms were apparent for a long time, but her behaviors had to worsen before the school system would listen and partner with her treatment plan. For many parents, this is a common struggle. **"I also want people to know that even if someone isn't showing signs, it still might be very serious,"** Tabara says. **"And there is lots of variation within each diagnosis."**

Her symptoms have always fluctuated, and many of them have lessened or gone away over time. But for a couple of years during grade school, Tabara would experience what she calls an **"emotional fit"**—emotions so intense that she would have mental blackouts. When the experience ended, Tabara would have no recollection of what had just occurred. This would leave her wondering why her mom or anyone else around her needed some breathing room. It was a challenging time between mother and daughter.

Tabara's depression can make her feel **"empty, drowning."** She can see a **"foreseeable way to fix it, but it's just out of reach. Like it should be easy to get out of bed, but it isn't."** There was also a time when her depression would leave her feeling so sad and empty that »

"Empty. Drowning."

she became reckless, doing **"stupid stuff,"** as she describes it.

Today she feels she's in **"a nice place, where my depression isn't so dark and sad."** She can better identify when she needs help from her mom to get out of a funk, such as when she's not showering for several days or not wanting to get out of bed.

Now that she isn't so weighed down by depression, Tabara wonders if she focuses more on her anxiety. In an instant, her emotions can fluctuate from feeling fine to having a panic attack. **"It sounds ominous, but when in the panic attack, it feels like I'm dying. I can't breathe. My heart beats faster. Even my brain is going faster. Thoughts are whooshing by faster than I can speak them."**

Tabara's friends have experienced her anxiety firsthand. **"I'd suddenly grab their arm for emotional support in a crowded hallway in school,"** she recalls. This experience has made her friends more understanding. **"I get it now,"** they've told her.

Tabara manages her depression and anxiety in a variety of ways. Art therapy is a tool she uses as needed. Taking medication **"helps keep me regulated,"** a lesson she learned when she stopped taking them for a while.

Talking with supportive friends and family also helps Tabara manage her feelings. **"It's easier for me to identify my feelings now than when I was younger,"** she says. However, one of the most difficult things is figuring out how to honestly describe her feelings without **"freaking out the adult who might think I need to be admitted [to a hospital]."** She must find a way to convey the seriousness of how she's feeling without **"making it sound too over-the-top."**

For those living with mental illness, Tabara urges them to seek professional help rather than go it alone. **"Trying to deal with things with essential oils and yoga is OK, but it's not a primary way to deal with really serious things. You need a mental health professional. It's not a bad thing. It's really important to get help."** She adds, **"Needing outside help doesn't mean you're crazy. Rather, you're a capable person—and that's a strength. I feel like I'm stronger today and better able to deal with things."** Again, she emphasizes how important it is to reach out: **"Isolation makes things worse!"**

Tammy, age 38
"The wall."

"I don't let anyone behind the wall, even those closest to me," Tammy says. She is a very private person who sometimes doesn't leave her home. In the interview, however, she reveals a glimpse of her life. Serious topics are discussed, but the conversation is also interspersed with wittiness and laughter.

Tammy lives with depression, anxiety, dissociative identity disorder (formerly known as multiple personality disorder), and schizoaffective disorder, as well as a traumatic brain injury likely caused by banging her head out of frustration. "I may look fine on the outside," she says, "but inside I feel like I melted and died."

Starting at age five, Tammy endured a series of sexual abuse by men in her life. In addition, her stepfather was verbally and mentally abusive. Life worsened for her after another molestation at sixteen.

In high school, Tammy was a loner but also a troublemaker who just wanted any attention to help her feel better. She was diagnosed with schizophrenia during this time. She attended an alternative school but couldn't stay focused. She was then transferred to a state hospital.

Dissociative disorders typically develop as a way to deal with overwhelming traumatic events. Due to her dissociative identity disorder, Tammy has five distinct personalities:

Gumic: She is five years old. She is the least powerful physically but the stablest when it comes to knowing what is healthy and understanding good versus bad.

Damian: He is eighteen and the only male identity. He thinks he's the most powerful. He's very controlling and is the cheerleader of doing bad things.

Tazlee: She is an eighteen-year-old drug addict. She is manipulative and demanding, but her influence is very small now. »

T: She is a teenager, about sixteen years old. She is very quiet—the innocent caretaker. She is the identity present about a third of the time.

Tammy: She is the dominant personality. Somewhat outgoing, she is the identity being interviewed for this project.

To cope with emotional pain and to quiet the voices—especially that of **"the guy,"** Damian—Tammy has and will still sometimes self-mutilate her arms and hands, often with a lit cigarette. The scars, old and new, serve as a visible testament to her lifelong emotional pain.

Tammy feels she didn't make any real progress in life until she began her relationship with her partner. Her emotional support helps keep Tammy on the straight and narrow. Tammy also takes her meds regularly, has social support, and sees a counselor. In addition, she expresses herself beautifully through poetry.

"Don't give up," she says to those living with mental illness. **"Things may be rough at times—they will get better. Give it time, even though it feels like it will take forever to get stable."** Tammy also wants you to understand that **"not everything you see or hear about mental illness is true. How mental illness is misjudged...People think they know everything about it, and that's not true."**

"The wall."

Teresa, age 59
"Endless barren road of ups and downs."

Teresa is an impressive woman filled with determination and humor. She lives with and manages major depression that feels like an **"endless barren road of ups and downs."**

Life is easier today because she can identify when the depression is coming. If she can, she'll confront her problem head on to avoid her life getting too out of control. But she also admits that the hardest thing for people to understand about her mental illness is that it's not her fault. **"I didn't ask to get depression. It just happened."**

Teresa encourages people living with mental illness to not be afraid to reach out. **"If you're reluctant to seek help, *seek help!*"** she urges. **"Get over the stigma of depression. 'Loony.' 'Nuts.' You're not! Get over these words. If you had a broken arm, you'd see a doctor. Depression is kind of like your brain is broken, so you see a professional for that too."**

Tina, age 56
"A big weight in my chest..."

"I didn't find anything funny," Tina says of her life with depression. **"And I didn't even look forward to things I really loved."** Tina's depression has felt like **"a big weight inside my chest, where it would feel like my whole body was heavy and would collapse."**

At her lowest point, she'd wake up with a horrible stomachache that would improve a bit by evening but then intensify by the next morning. During one of Tina's worst panic attacks, she was shaking and sweating from the pressure of having to make crucial decisions about her life. Despite it all, she always had **"this constant desire to get better *right* away!"**

In the past, Tina denied her clinical depression and anxiety diagnoses by blaming them on external happenings in her life. Today, though, she's more open to managing the ebb and flow of her mental illness through a variety of tools: light therapy, exercise, talk therapy,

mindfulness, and making an effort to be social. Setting up structured activities in her day-to-day life helps her focus less on her symptoms, which enables her to keep the depression at bay or come out of it sooner. Medication has also been an important tool ever since the time when her depression and anxiety significantly worsened. **"I didn't feel like I was getting through it. The talk therapy just wasn't enough."**

Many people don't realize that a person can be suffering on the inside despite appearing high functioning and happy on the outside. This misconception can be heard in negative comments such as "I thought you were so tough," "Just pick yourself up by your bootstraps," and "You can't be that bad because you don't look it." Tina heard these types of comments from others and even made them about herself. She admits, **"I struggle sometimes with the same prejudices—about myself—and** »

I try not to judge others with mental illness."

Tina acknowledges the impact mental illness has on her life. For instance, she doesn't always know when her symptoms will worsen. **"It makes it really hard to plan and commit to future events,"** she says. **"I ultimately don't want to disappoint people."** Still, she has found a way to live through this uncertainty. She is proud to declare that she has traveled to Nicaragua, become a dean at a college, and moved halfway across the country. **"I did the things I did *despite* my anxiety and depression."**

Postscript

With one in five people experiencing a mental illness, the need for understanding is paramount. There should be no shame nor need to keep it hidden. No one keeps diabetes or arthritis a secret. Yet people who have been diagnosed with mental illness are often reluctant to share this with friends, family, and coworkers for fear of rejection and ridicule.

One solution: listen. If a friend, family member, or coworker tells you they have mental illness, just listen and talk to them. (Mostly just listen.) This is what you'd want if the tables were turned, right? Nothing has inherently changed about this person just because you have this new piece of information. It's not contagious. No one with mental illness chooses to have it. Mental illness can happen anytime to anyone.

And that person *could* be you.

I can't escape that this photo essay is ultimately my interpretation of other people's experiences living with mental illness. I've thought a lot about my creative process for this project, and I realized how important it was that you see and hear everyone through my lens both literally and figuratively. It's important that you see their strength and determination (even when they may not see it themselves). I don't want you to see mental illness. I want you to see a *person*.

Some might say the goals of *If You Only Knew* are too lofty: to decrease discrimination, increase awareness about the experience of mental illness, and ultimately to humanize it. But if this book resonates with just one person—either by validating their own experience with mental illness or by helping them understand others' experiences with mental illness—then the goals will have been met.

I've seen firsthand the difference *If You Only Knew* has made. Over a year ago, I observed a fleeting but powerful moment at the opening art reception for the exhibit's debut. (I tear up every time I tell this story.) From across the room and unbeknown to Tammy, I happened to notice her expression as she looked at her part of the exhibit. Her face quietly beamed with pride.

If you read her interview, you know Tammy has experienced things no human should, and as a result is often very quiet, anxious, and withdrawn. I didn't foresee such a reaction from her, nor did I foresee the positive impact this project would have on her.

That is a moment I'll never forget.

Barb Kellogg
Avon, Minnesota
9-18-19

Resources

Note: The resources listed below are not intended to be a comprehensive list and were accurate at the time of this writing.

Mental Health Resources

- American Academy of Child and Adolescent Psychiatry: aacap.org
- National Alliance on Mental Illness: nami.org
- National Institute of Mental Health: nimh.nih.gov

Help Lines within the United States

- In an emergency: dial 911 and notify the operator that it is a psychiatric emergency
- National Suicide Prevention Lifeline: call 1-800-273-TALK (8255)
- Crisis Text Line: text HOME to 741741

Help Line within Canada

- Crisis Text Line: text HOME to 686868

Help Line within the United Kingdom

- Shout / Crisis Text Line: text SHOUT to 85258

International Resources

- Psychology Today: psychologytoday.com/us. Provides a search for therapists and support groups in the United States and countries in western Europe, Canada, Australia, and New Zealand. From the menu bar, click on the globe icon to the far right, and select your country from the drop-down menu.
- International Association for Suicide Prevention: iasp.info/Provides suicide prevention resources, guides, and information.

About the Author

Barb Kellogg, an award-winning fine art nature photographer, became an accidental author when she pursued the creation of the photo essay *If You Only Knew*. An example of life coming full circle, her current passion for photography merged with her past education in psychology and human development.

Her artistic journey has evolved to create photographic imagery that is *about* something, not *of* something. She often asks herself, "What do I want this image to feel like?" Photography gives her the freedom to express emotions, much like an actor in a play. She finds it liberating and therapeutic to create images that span the emotional spectrum.

Barb and her husband live in Avon, Minnesota. To learn more about Barb Kellogg, please visit www.barbkellogg.com.

www.ingramcontent.com/pod-product-compliance
Lightning Source LLC
Chambersburg PA
CBHW041242020426
42333CB00003B/55

* 9 7 8 1 9 4 6 1 9 5 5 0 0 *